STONEHENGE

The Mysteries of England's Most Sacred Historical Landmark

Phil Coleman

Table of Contents

Mystery and Intrigue

Mention Stonehenge and many people instantly think of an ancient monument with religious significance. They see images of Druids at sunrise, the summer and winter solstices, and festivals.

There are hundreds of ancient circles around the UK — an estimated 900 now and possibly over 4,000 at one time. The earliest ones were built of wood but that changed to stone in the late Neolithic and early Bronze Age period. Stonehenge may, therefore, be regarded as just one amongst many.

It is, however, without doubt unique. It's a wonderful piece of engineering, especially considering it was built by people who had only the most rudimentary of tools to do the

job. Its history goes back over 4,500 years —
even older than the Egyptian pyramids —
and possibly even further, with evidence of
other major construction on the site going
back another 2,000 years. Indeed, some large
Mesolithic post holes found under the
current car park are dated around 8,000 BC,
indicating a possible 10,000 year plus usage
of the site.

Stonehenge is located in the county of
Wiltshire, two miles to the west of
Amesbury, with Salisbury about eight miles
to the north. It's considered to be the most
important historical monument in the UK
and has been legally protected as a
Scheduled Ancient Monument since 1882.

The first written mention of Stonehenge was
in the Twelfth Century when historian and

explorer Henry of Huntingdon described the features of 'Stonenges'. Even then, however, he was speculating how and why it was built. Subsequent writing referred to the monument as 'Stanhenge', 'Stonhenge', the 'stone hegles' and finally, by 1610, Stonehenge as we know it today.

The word 'henge' generally refers to an earthwork of the Neolithic period. The name Stonehenge, therefore, likely derives from the later development of the site when standing stones were added to the previous earthwork construction. There are also references to 'hanging stones, or 'supported stones' to justify the name, while others point to the fact that the lintels 'hinge' onto the upright stones.

Changing Ownership of Stonehenge

King Henry VIII acquired Amesbury Abbey and surrounding land, including Stonehenge, but ownership has changed numerous times since then. He gave the estate to the Earl of Hertford in 1540, who later passed it on to Lord Carleton. From him, it went to the Marquis of Queensbury and, in 1824, was bought by the Antrobus family of Cheshire.

After the last heir to the family was killed in World War I, Stonehenge and surrounding land were sold at auction on 21st September 1915. The property was bought for £6,600 by Cecil Chubb, apparently as a whim because he thought the site should be locally owned. He donated Stonehenge to the government three years later, on condition that it would be cared for properly and would be open for public visits, and was knighted as a result.

By the late 1920s, the development of modern buildings in the immediate vicinity was threatening Stonehenge and a nationwide appeal was launched to save it. The donations that resulted enabled the surrounding land to be bought and given to the National Trust, which removed the buildings and returned the land to agricultural use. This process is now being taken a step further, the land being restored to open grassland as it was when Stonehenge was built.

Stonehenge is now owned by the Crown and managed by English Heritage. The surrounding land continues to be owned and managed by the National Trust.

Controversies and Questions Still Go On

Some 3,500 years after the development of Stonehenge came to an end, and after a long period of deterioration in the intervening period, it, at last, seemed the site was safe for the future. However, there still remain controversies about the way the site and surrounding landscape are maintained and managed, as well as the inevitable questions that have surrounded Stonehenge for many years.

Despite all the research undertaken and the countless thousands of words written about Stonehenge, more questions than answers still remain. Why and how was it built? What was its purpose? And why, after so many years, does it still hold a magical attraction to so many people?

Whilst some of these questions have been answered to a degree, there are contrasting theories and the jury is still out in a lot of cases. However, this does all add to the intrigue that surrounds Stonehenge and will keep archaeologists and researchers occupied for many years to come.

Stonehenge remains a majestic spectacle that dominates the surrounding landscape. It is a truly awe-inspiring construction, created by hundreds of people working together with primitive tools and technologies. Despite the impressive nature of their achievement, however, the spiritual and inspirational aura of the place remains the dominant impression.

Features of the Site Today

The centrepiece of Stonehenge is the stone circle, comprising a number of standing stones, some of which have stone lintels. Surrounding these stones are a circular earth bank and ditch, believed to be the results of the earliest stages of construction here.

The stone circle comprises an inner and outer arrangement of stones, being either sarsen stones (a type of sandstone) that have an average weight of 25 tons and the smaller bluestones that weigh between two and five tons each. Although the bluestones aren't really blue, they have a bluish tinge when wet. There are 83 stones in total.

The sarsens were erected as an inner horseshoe pattern surrounded by an outer circle. The horseshoe comprises five trilithons (two vertical stones with a horizontal lintel on top), of which two are partly fallen whilst three still stand. One of the latter fell in 1797 but was re-erected in 1958. A fallen stone from the tallest trilithon partly covers the Altar Stone, which is at the centre of the horseshoe.

The stones comprising the trilithons are the largest of all, weighing up to fifty tons each. They are arranged symmetrically and linked by complex jointing. Some of the stones have carvings of axe heads and daggers, thought to be Bronze Age weapons.

The outer circle surrounds the horseshoe. It originally comprised thirty sarsen stones, all capped with lintels, although many of the stones have fallen and some stones and lintels are missing. Only seventeen of the sarsen stones still stand and each is about thirteen feet (4.1 metres) high and six foot eleven inches (2.1 metres) wide.

A number of the sarsen stones were brought down during the Roman occupation of Britain while three stones fell in 1797 and two others in 1900, the latter five stones then being re-erected in 1958. Within the sarsens are a circle and inner oval comprised of bluestones. Some of these have now fallen, while others are missing and a number are only stumps.

One of the most significant features of the stones, which help to make Stonehenge unique in terms of the construction of the monument, is the way they fit together. The lintels were fitted on to the standing stones using mortise holes and protruding tenons while the lintels were joined by tongue and groove joints, a technique more usually found in woodworking.

The Surrounding Bank and Ditch

Surrounding the stones are a circular earth bank and a ditch that enclosed the site. To the north east was the main entrance with a smaller one in the south. There are several more gaps today due to later tracks created across the site.

The Avenue, a twelve-metre wide corridor marked today by low banks, connects the entrance to the River Avon. Outside the main entrance is the Heel Stone, a large unshaped sarsen boulder and the largest stone of all at about thirty tons that originally had an accompanying stone near it. Anyone standing in the inner circle at the summer solstice will see the sun rise over the Heel Stone.

Also near the entrance is the Slaughter Stone, sixteen feet (4.9 metres) long and now fallen, which was so-called because it was believed to have been used as a place for human sacrifice. Four Station Stones, only two of which remain, marked the corners of a rectangle and are thought to relate to the solstice alignment or the original setting out of Stonehenge.

Within the enclosed area are 56 pits, known as the 'Aubrey Holes' after John Aubrey who first discovered them in the late Seventeenth Century. Some of these were found to contain cremation burials, reflecting the area's first use as a cemetery site, although there are suggestions the holes were originally created to support a bluestone standing circle.

The latest additions to the Stonehenge site, in 2014, are replica Neolithic houses that have been constructed behind the visitor centre. These were built using authentic materials and techniques, having wattle and dung walls surmounted by steeply pitched thatched roofs. They are intended to illustrate to visitors how people lived 4,500 years ago but have not been universally welcomed, adding to the controversy that has seemingly always surrounded Stonehenge.

The Significance of Stonehenge

Stonehenge's unique position as a prehistoric monument site of great significance was recognised by it being awarded, in 1986 along with nearby Avebury, World Heritage status. It was one of the first sites in the UK to go on the UNESCO World Heritage list.

Accompanying the award is a World Heritage Site Management Plan that indicates the importance of the site by stating:

"The Stonehenge, Avebury, and Associated Sites World Heritage Site is internationally important for its complexes of outstanding prehistoric monuments. Stonehenge is the most architecturally sophisticated prehistoric stone circle in the world, while Avebury is the largest in the world. Together with inter-related monuments and their associated landscapes, they help us to understand Neolithic and Bronze Age ceremonial and mortuary practices. They demonstrate around 2000 years of continuous use and monument building between c. 3700 and 1600 BC. As such they represent a unique embodiment of our collective heritage."

The significance of the site comes from various features that include the huge difficulties presented in the transport of the materials and their construction, and the sophisticated techniques that were used. It remains the only surviving lintelled stone circle in the world and was one of the largest cremation cemeteries in Neolithic Britain in the early stages of its development. It's also within an area that contains numerous other monuments and burial mounds from the Neolithic and Bronze Age period, so it is a vital archaeological feature for that period.

The fame and significance of any important site can often be judged in terms of the number of later versions there are around the world. In the case of Stonehenge, there are replicas in Australia and New Zealand, a World War I memorial in Washington State that resembles the monument, and even 'Carhenge' in Nebraska where there are cars in place of stones.

Lessons Still to be Learned

Stonehenge and surrounding sites provide crucial information about how archaeology developed, how people lived and how society was organised at that time. Even today, it has a role as a place with religious and cultural significance, and is still somewhere for ceremonies and celebrations.

Continuous research and excavations have significantly increased the understanding of why and how it was built and how it was used. New techniques have accelerated the rate of learning about Stonehenge and will ensure that knowledge continues to grow and evolve.

How Stonehenge Was Developed

Given its size and complexity, coupled with the lack of sophisticated techniques and tools available at the time it was constructed, Stonehenge continues to be regarded as a marvel of engineering. Those who originally studied the site were at first baffled as to how, with limited resources, Neolithic people could transport, shape and erect stones of such size.

The main resources were the ingenuity of the designers and the sheer weight of manpower that was available, working as a team to get the job done. That job was spread over many hundreds of years, with the first development widely thought to have started around 3000 BC and construction ending in 1600 BC or thereabouts.

There is, however, some evidence of construction starting much earlier, due to post holes being detected that date from 8000 BC. A causewayed enclosure, at Robin Hood's Ball, and a Stonehenge Cursus (a length of parallel banks with external ditches) were both constructed about 2,300 feet (700 metres) north of the site in 3500 BC.

It is generally accepted that the real start of the main construction for Stonehenge was around 3000 BC and continued until 1500 BC, a total construction phase of 1,500 years. One estimate is that almost 30 million hours of labour would have been needed to extract, transport, shape and erect the stones.

Although construction has variously been attributed to the Romans, the Danes, the Mycenae people from the Aegean Sea area and others, the most widely accepted theory is that Stonehenge was built by the Druids, a priestly caste of Celts who kept the lore of the Celts and led their ceremonial rites. However, this doesn't altogether fit in with the dating of the site's construction and so the identity of the builders remains something of a mystery to this day.

The First Phase of Development

The first major development, in 3000 BC, was the construction of the circular earthwork enclosure. A ditch was dug using tools made from antlers and the chalk soil that was excavated was used to form the inner and outer banks. Although the ditch was continuous, it had been dug in sections, suggesting that different groups had been responsible for each section.

Deer and oxen bones plus some flint tools were found at the bottom of the ditch. These were well cared for and were older than the antlers that were used to dig the ditch. It is believed that they might have been placed there deliberately to indicate the end of an era and a change in the direction of development.

The structure was about 360 feet (110 metres) in diameter, with a ditch that was some six feet (two metres) deep, and stood in open grassland that sloped slightly. The main entrance was to the north east, with a smaller one to the south, and the earthworks enclosed the so-called 'Aubrey Holes'.

A 2013 excavation, led by Professor Mike Parker Pearson, discovered the cremated bones of 63 individuals in a single hole. These had been placed there from a previous excavation in 1920 that had found them in the Aubrey Holes and relocated them. They provided evidence of the use of Stonehenge as a burial site over a period of five centuries, from 3000 BC to 2500 BC.

The outer bank of the earthworks has largely been ploughed away over the years. The inner bank and ditch remain and are visible as low earthworks in the grass.

Transformation of the Site

The next major change to the site was the building of the stone circles, which occurred in about 2500 BC. This was a significant development since it marked a complete change of construction materials, from wood to stone. Compared to the construction of the earthworks, it was a monumental task since it involved the sourcing, movement, preparation and erection of several gigantic stones.

It is widely accepted that the larger sarsen stones come from the Marlborough Downs, about twenty miles away, where large quantities of these stones can still be found. The smaller bluestones, however, come from much further away, with the Preseli Hills in south west Wales thought to be the most likely source. The large Altar Stone is believed to have originated from the Brecon Beacons in South Wales.

A bluestone quarry at Craig Rhos-y-felin in Pembrokeshire has been identified as the probable origin of the stones. This, however, is 150 miles (240 kilometres) from Stonehenge and would have presented immense logistical problems in transporting the heavy stones over such a great distance.

The Task of Transporting the Stones

One theory, pronounced by a team of Welsh researchers, is that the stones were actually moved naturally by glaciers over 500,000 years ago. They argue that holes cut into the rock face at the Preseli Hills quarry, which some have claimed match the stones at Stonehenge, are instead a natural formation or may have been caused by archaeological activity.

Another suggestion, put forward by Professor Mike Parker Pearson, is that Stonehenge resulted from a monument that was originally constructed in Wales and then moved to its new site many years later. Evidence presented for this includes radio carbon dating of the rock holes at the quarry that appear to have been made 300-500 years before Stonehenge was built and the fact that 500,000 bone fragments found at Stonehenge appear to come from people who originated from the west of Britain, possibly from Wales.

There is the belief that the bluestones at Stonehenge may be able to be matched to the rock face at the quarry in the Preseli Hills and a dig is planned to find the site of the original Welsh tomb. Some work undertaken so far suggests that the stones were cut from the quarry many years before Stonehenge was built, adding weight to the theory that they were first used elsewhere.

Professor Pearson thinks the re-siting of the monument was part of a move from Wales to establish a base further east, possibly in an effort to unite warring tribes. That involved not only moving people and their belongings, but also the physical embodiment of their ancestors in the form of their remains and the tomb where they had been interred. If this is true, it suggests that the Neolithic people's culture and religion were based on worshipping their ancestral dead.

How the Stones Were Obtained and Moved

The most widely accepted theory is that the bluestones were mined at the quarry in Wales and then transported to Stonehenge. The extraction process involved inserting wooden wedges in the cracks between pillars, then letting rain swell the wood and crack the stone so it could be removed.

The transfer from Wales is likely to have been a long and tortuous process that involved sections on land and water. The first stage would have probably been to Milford Haven, where the stones would have been loaded onto rafts. From there, they would have proceeded along the South Wales coast before coming up the River Avon and the River Frome. They could then have been dragged overland to a point near Warminster in Wiltshire, where they would have gone back onto rafts to be transported along the River Wye to Salisbury, and then along the River Avon to West Amesbury.

Rather than the straight line distance of 150 miles, this route would have covered almost 240 miles. Movement of the stones on land is likely to have been on sledges or rollers. One experiment in 1995 involved a team of one hundred people pulling a forty-ton slab for eighteen miles on a sleight running on a track greased with animal fat, proving this method of transport was a possibility.

Estimates have been put forward that 500 men using leather ropes could have been needed to pull one stone, with a further 100 men required to position the rollers ahead of the sledge. Alternatively, it has been suggested that teams of oxen may have been used to haul the stones.

The sarsen stones were also no doubt dragged to site using rollers or sledges and, although the distance was significantly less, the weight was many times greater. An alternative method would have been to carry some of the stones on frameworks of poles, which might have been possible for the smaller stones that weighed up to two tons, but not for the massive standing stones.

Preparing and Erecting the Stones

Once on site, the stones had to be worked to the required shape using hammer stones. Large hammer stones were used to chip away parts of the stone and then smaller ones gave a smooth finish to the surface. Not all the stones were finished to the same standard, those on the north east side and the inner faces of the central trilithons being more finely dressed.

A number of broken hammer stones and quantities of waste material from sarsen stones and bluestones have been found in fields to the north of Stonehenge. This rather proves that the shaping of the stones was undertaken there and casts doubt on theories that the stones were originally erected elsewhere and then moved, as well as other more bizarre speculation.

The last task was to erect the stones into their final positions, which was another extremely challenging job. The likely method was to dig a large hole with a sloping edge at the front and a row of wooden stakes at the rear. The stone would then be pulled into the hole, probably using a combination of a wooden A-frame and ropes made from plant fibre.

Weights may also have been used to bring the stones into an upright position. Once properly in place, the stones would be held upright by packing each hole with rubble.

Each standing stone would have a tenon carved at the top while the lintel to be placed on it would have a mortise hole that would be precisely cut and shaped to ensure a good fit. Each lintel was shaped with a curve to the outer edge to ensure a true circle was formed.

The lintels were probably raised onto the standing stones with the aid of timber platforms. Tests have shown that it would have been possible to push the lintels up ramps using levers to move the stones and timbers to hold them in place, until the lintels reached the timber platforms and could then be pushed into their final position.

The tongue and groove joints that connected the lintels, like the mortise and tenon joints, were precisely cut to fit correctly. Signs of these joints are still visible today on some of the stones.

The last detected development at Stonehenge, thought to be between 1600 and 1500 BC, was the digging of a ring of pits that are referred to as the Y holes. These surround another ring of pits, known as the Z holes, that encircle the sarsen stones and were dug somewhat earlier. The purpose of both sets of pits is unknown.

Although the Stonehenge we see today is not the same as the one built over 3,500 years ago, the fact that so much of it remains is a testament to the skill and persistence of those who created it. Much of their work is still evident and it remains a source of wonder to those who see it.

Stonehenge's Purpose

Whilst the question of how Stonehenge was built has fascinated people for centuries, the reasons for its construction have been an equal source of conjecture. It is widely accepted that one of the earliest uses was as a burial ground due to the large number of cremated remains found on the site.

Stonehenge is known to have been the largest cemetery in Britain during the third millennium, with the burials occurring over a 500 year period between 3000 BC and 2500 BC. Some experts believe the dead were brought along the River Severn and then carried to Stonehenge, probably along the Stonehenge Avenue in a grand procession before cremation and then burial.

Was Stonehenge a Domain of the Dead?

One suggestion, by Professor Mike Parker Pearson, is that Stonehenge was a domain of the dead and nearby Durrington Walls was a place for the living. The deceased would be taken on a ritual passage from life to death, from the avenue at Durrington Walls to the River Avon, and then from the Avon to Stonehenge via another avenue there. This fits in with findings at both of the sites and also with stone henges sometimes being known as 'stone gallows' since they marked the end of life and formed a gateway where humans could return to their origins.

Although burial is known to be the earliest use of the site, it is not necessarily the original purpose of its construction and conflicting theories remain. One of the biggest problems is that the builders of the monument left no written records and so theories can only be expounded based on excavations and research.

One theory, which fits in with the large number of burials and the fact that some of the deceased were believed to have trauma deformity, is that Stonehenge was a place of healing. This theory was put forward by Professor Geoffrey Wainwright, president of the Society of Antiquaries, and Timothy Darvill of Bournemouth University, who believe that Stonehenge could have been the primaeval equivalent of Lourdes today. Weight is lent to this belief by analysis that shows some of the remains found at Stonehenge were of people from other parts of Europe.

An Observatory, Concert Hall or Something Else?

The alignment of the stones, with the open end of the horseshoe-shaped ones lined up with the points of sunrise for the summer solstice and sunset during the winter solstice, has led many to believe that Stonehenge was designed as an early form of observatory. This could well have allowed people to track and predict each equinox and other celestial events such as eclipses, which were important for their religious needs.

This is the explanation that is most favoured by English Heritage, the site's operator, which notes that Stonehenge is most probably a prehistoric temple aligned with the movements of the sun. One theory put forward by Geoffrey of Monmouth in the

Twelfth Century, is that Stonehenge was built as a monument to hundreds of Britons who were slain by the Saxons.

In addition to the alignment of the stones with the midsummer sunrise and the midwinter sunset, Stonehenge is also said to have a perfect geometric construction. All aspects of the stones — height, weight, orientation, scope and distance apart — are reckoned to be mathematically configured and therefore demonstrate an intimate knowledge of geometry. This leads some to believe that Stonehenge was built with mathematics in mind.

Another suggestion, made by several researchers, is that Stonehenge was a form of early concert hall. This is based on the fact that the stones, due to their shape and size, create excellent acoustics by enhancing the sound of music and voices. Striking the stones has also been found to produce a loud clanging noise.

These acoustic properties would, of course, have been more than useful for the conduct of rituals. They may also help to explain why the bluestones were brought so far for use in the construction, since they were believed to be sourced from near Maenclochog in Wales, a name meaning 'ringing rock' in Welsh, which partly explains their acoustic properties. The bluestones were thought by many to have healing powers, which supports the theory that Stonehenge was a place of healing.

Ceremonial or Unification Purpose

There have been suggestions that Stonehenge might have been a ceremonial location where Danish kings were crowned or even that ancient alien visitors constructed a model of the solar system there. Another alternative is that it was the subject of an exercise to bring people together.

It was built at a time when the Neolithic peoples of Britain were undergoing increased unification so construction could have been intended to demonstrate this unity since it required the constructive co-operation of a large number of people over long distances and a lengthy period. The people then were thought to be undergoing a period of cultural unification, so Stonehenge may have been built as a symbol of that.

No site that attracts so much attention for so long could possibly escape the attention of the extraterrestrial theorists and Stonehenge is no exception. Some believe it was a landing pad for aliens from space in ancient times. Indeed, there have been several reports of UFOs being sighted near the monument.

Discounting the more bizarre suggestions, it is widely accepted that Stonehenge has had several functions over its long history. The likelihood is that its use as a burial site was tied in with religious rituals, which were in turn connected with the movement of the sun and other planets.

The Solstice and Religious Festivals

Whatever Stonehenge's original and subsequent purposes, what cannot be denied is that its construction is aligned with the movement of the sun and it seems highly likely that this is no coincidence.

The main aspects of the monument — the horseshoe formation of the main five trilithons, the Heal Stone and the Avenue that leads to the River Avon — are aligned to the sunrise of the summer solstice and the sunset of the winter solstice. As recently as 2004, two huge pits were discovered within the South Cursus that are also aligned with the midsummer sunrise and sunset in a line from the Heel Stone.

Sunrise in midsummer is from a north east direction and occurs almost over the Heel Stone. Conversely, sunset at mid-winter is in the south-west, in the gap between the two tallest trilithons, although one of these is no longer standing. The north east entrance, which was widened around 2600 BC when the standing stones were erected, precisely matches the sunrise in mid-summer and the sunset in mid-winter.

Significance of the Solstices

The word 'solstice' is derived from 'solstitium', a Latin word that refers to the stopping of the movement of the sun. The summer solstice, generally 21st June in the northern hemisphere, marks the date the sun reaches its furthest point northwards and is the longest day of the year, with daylight exceeding 16.5 hours in the UK.

The winter solstice, on the other hand, is the shortest day of the year, usually 21st December, after which the sun starts to move north again. The spring and autumn equinoxes occur between these two dates, generally 21st March and 21st September, and indicate when the sun is directly over the equator on its journey north or south respectively.

The most important of these dates for various religious orders is the summer solstice. For pagans, in particular, it marks the union of their god and goddess and was used as a marker on which the planting and harvesting of crops was based.

The summer solstice at Stonehenge is most particularly associated with Druids, who turn up in large numbers before dawn each year to celebrate the occasion. This became especially popular in the Twentieth Century when neo-Druids and others following New Age beliefs began to increasingly treat Stonehenge as a place of great religious significance.

In August 1905, the Ancient Order of Druids held a mass initiation ceremony at the monument, admitting 259 new members to the order. The ceremony was widely ridiculed at the time due to the participants wearing fake beards and flowing white robes. The consumption of large quantities of alcohol by the 700 or so people present did not help to portray the event as a serious ceremony.

The Stonehenge Free Festival and the Battle of the Beanfield

The popularity of rituals at the summer solstice grew from 1972 through to 1984, when the Stonehenge Free Festival was held. This was attended by an increasing number of revellers, as many as 30,000 in its final year, who celebrated the longest day of the year.

The Stonehenge Free Festival ended after 1984 due to the site being closed to revellers by English Heritage and the National Trust, partly due to pressure from local landowners who were concerned about unruly behaviour. Nevertheless, at the summer solstice in 1985, a collection of New Age travellers and others, who regularly attended various festivals in an assembly known as the Convoy, tried to visit Stonehenge as in previous years to hold the festival.

With the help of police helicopter support, the Convoy was tracked to a bean field in Wiltshire. The revellers were confronted there by riot police to prevent them accessing the Stonehenge site and the resulting violent outcome became widely known as the Battle of the Beanfield.

Up until 1977, visitors to Stonehenge had been allowed to walk among the stones without restriction. However, this led to serious concerns about erosion and damage, particularly as a result of people climbing on the stones. Consequently, restrictions were imposed by roping off the stones so they could only be viewed from a short distance away.

Limited Access Permitted

Access to the stones is still permitted by special permission and during the period of the summer and winter solstices. For a period of fifteen years after the Battle of the Beanfield, there was no access to the stones at all. As a consequence, Druids were reduced to holding their celebrations within sight of the stones, at the side of the busy road.

This changed just before the end of the Twentieth Century, partly as a result of a concerted campaign by various Druid representatives, including a campaigner know as King Arthur Pendragon. The Court of Human Rights ruled that members of religions can worship in their own church and, since neo-Druids, Pagans and others regarded Stonehenge as their place of worship, they should be allowed access.

As a result of this ruling, limited access to the stones is now allowed four times a year, at the summer and winter solstices as well as the spring and autumn equinoxes. Consequent to this, numbers attending have risen again, with an estimated 30,000 people in attendance in 2003 when the summer solstice occurred on a weekend.

The current solstice festivities are not free from the problems of modern life, however. As a result of various terrorist attacks, armed police are now to be deployed at the site as part of an increase in security at all major festivals and other events. The security measures, which are likely to be a feature in future, also include limits on bag sizes and the searching of festival goers.

Other Monuments with Similar Purposes

Stonehenge is not unique in respect of its celestial significance. Indeed, there are hundreds of stone monuments within Britain. These include Scotland's Callanish Stones on the Isle of Lewis and the Standing Stones of Stenness on the Isle of Orkney, which were built over 5,000 years ago.

Research has shown that the stones in these circles are placed to coincide with the paths of the sun and moon at different cyclic points. As well as their alignment with the sunrise and sunset, the stone circles are aligned with the most northerly rising and most southerly setting of the moon. Their arrangement is such that the stones can be used to predict the appearance of the moon at its most northerly point, which only takes place every 18.6 years.

These stones are considered to be important to Neolithic people for their beliefs. As part of this, they needed to be able to determine when the days were starting to shorten and when the sun was starting its journey north and warmer days were coming.

Since the structures are somewhat simpler than Stonehenge, the aim is to complete the investigation of these first to fully discover their secrets. After that, the intention is to move on to Stonehenge where the alignments are much more varied and the challenges are more complex due to the monument being built in several stages.

Research and Excavations of Stonehenge

In view of the complexity and significance of Stonehenge, and its development over a long period, it is hardly surprising it has experienced a number of excavations and investigations. The aim of these has been partly to settle the speculation and numerous theories that have arisen due to the mystery surrounding the site as a result of the lack of records left by its developers and users.

Excavations since 1620

The earliest known of these excavations was undertaken in the 1620s by the Duke of Buckingham after a visit to Stonehenge by

King James. A survey by architect Indigo Jones, at the request of King James, followed soon after and Jones' conclusion was that the monument was constructed by the Romans.

Around 1666, antiquarian John Aubrey surveyed the site and discovered the 56 pits that were subsequently named the 'Aubrey Holes' in recognition of his find. These pits were each about three feet wide and deep, forming a circle that was 284 feet in diameter.

As a result of studying other stone circles, he concluded that Stonehenge had not been built by the Romans, as Indigo Jones had thought, nor by the Danes, as proposed by others, but by native inhabitants. He instead decided the Druids were responsible since they were the only British priests mentioned in texts of the time.

William Stukeley was next to survey the site, in the early Eighteenth Century, and he agreed with Aubrey that the Druids were responsible for its construction. His investigation was somewhat more wide-ranging, enabling him to identify the Avenue, Cursus and various barrows (burial mounds formed from earth and stones).

In 1740, Bath architect John Wood produced the most comprehensive and accurate plan to-date. His plan included the south west trilithon, which fell in 1797 and was re-elected in 1958.

William Cunnington excavated 24 barrows in the early Nineteenth Century, discovering ancient artefacts and identifying the hole where the Slaughter Stone had stood. A further 379 barrows on Salisbury Plain were excavated by Richard Colt Hoare.

Flinders Petrie surveyed Stonehenge in 1874 and again in 1877, setting up a numbering system for the stones that is still used today. Also in 1877, Charles Darwin, as part of his research into the long-term effect earthworms had on objects in the soil, determined that stones had fallen and then sunk deeper into the ground as a result of their activities. His conclusions were included in his book The Formation of Vegetable Mould Through the Action of Worms.

Twentieth Century and The Start of Restorations

The first restoration of any significance at Stonehenge took pace in 1901 after one of the sarsen stones and its lintel had fallen. This led to concerns over the stability of other stones, resulting in a large, leaning sarsen being straightened and concreted in place. In the course of this work, which was overseen by Professor William Gowland, it was concluded the monument was built in the late Neolithic or early Bronze Age period.

Further excavation and restoration work was undertaken during the period 1919 to 1926, directed by Lieutenant Colonel William Hawley, when much of the south east part of Stonehenge was excavated. During this process, he excavated the base of six stones and the outer ditch and helped re-locate the Aubrey Holes. Hawley reportedly found the whole process somewhat frustrating, complaining that the mystery seemed to deepen the further the excavation progressed.

In 1923, an excavation uncovered the skeleton of a decapitated man. All previously found remains were of cremated bodies from the Neolithic period whereas this was a Seventh Century Anglo-Saxon. Whilst the beheading suggested he might have been an executed criminal, the fact he was buried at Stonehenge could indicate he was a powerful person, even royalty.

A new campaign of excavations was undertaken during the period 1950 to 1964, by Professor Richard Atkinson, Stuart

Piggott and JF Stone. This was intended to resolve some outstanding questions and also to stabilise some features and re-erect others. A number of axes and knives were discovered and the work enabled the three separate phases of Stonehenge's development to be identified.

This period saw the re-erection of a fallen sarsen stone in 1958, which was set in a concrete base to ensure future stability. Five years later, another sarsen stone fell over and was concreted back into place along with a further three stones.

In preparation for the building of new visitor facilities, further excavations in 1966-7 revealed the post hole where a partner stone to the Heel Stone had been. Also found were various Mesolithic post holes, in one of which the 'Stonehenge Archer' was discovered in 1978. These remains were dated at 2300 BC, making the person a contemporary of the 'Amesbury Archer', buried around three miles away.

A Stonehenge Environs Project, conducted in the early 1980s, studied the surrounding landscape and was able to date various features that included the Lesser Cursus and the Coneybury Henge. A Public Accounts Committee conclusion in 1993 that Stonehenge's presentation to the public was a 'national disgrace' prompted English Heritage to bring together all the work conducted at the site so far. This led to the publication, in 1995, of Stonehenge in its landscape, setting out details of all items found at the site.

New Millennium Findings

A series of excavations led by Professor Mike Parker Pearson and known collectively as the Stonehenge Riverside Project took place between 2003 and 2008. The focus was on other nearby monuments and their relationship to Stonehenge. This involved excavations at Durrington Walls and Stonehenge and the discovery of further stones.

The project also, in 2008, removed cremated remains from some of the Aubrey Holes, analysis showing they were buried between 3000 and 2500 BC. That same year, Tim Darvill of the University of Bournemouth and Geoffrey Wainwright of the Society of Antiquaries began excavations within the stone circle. This enabled them to date some of the bluestones as being erected in 2300 BC and they also discovered organic material dating from 7000 BC.

The latter investigation was part of the SPACES (Strumble-Preseli Ancient Communities and Environmental Study) project that investigated the bluestone settings in order to establish the exact origin of the bluestones. As well as including geological analysis of the bluestones, there was also some fieldwork in the Preseli Hills.

Excavations during this period also found evidence of Roman activity at the site. Other excavations over many years have uncovered various Roman coins, metal items and pieces of pottery.

A further landscape investigation in 2009 identified a shallow mound that was thought to have been part of the original monument. A Stonehenge Hidden Landscape Project discovered, in 2010, a henge-like monument less than one mile from the main site and the following year found two huge pits within the Stonehenge Cursus pathway. These pits were aligned towards midsummer sunrise and sunset when seen from the Heel Stone.

Since the southwestern part of the sarsen stone circle lacks several stones, archaeologists and historians have long puzzled over whether it had been left incomplete or whether some stones had been removed after the circle's completion. This question was resolved, not by an excavation, but by a drought in 2014 that revealed marks in the grass that showed the position where stones had previously been.

As recently as 2014, evidence of adjacent stone and wooden structures and burial mounds, dating back to 4000 BC, was found by the University of Birmingham. Discoveries are therefore still being made so that the secrets of Stonehenge are slowly but surely being revealed.

Unresolved Questions Still Remain

Many questions still remain to be answered by future excavations and research projects. These include why Stonehenge was built on that particular site and the exact source of the stones. There are also outstanding questions about the methods and sequence of construction and whether the sarsen stone circle was ever completed.

Research has been complicated by periglacial movement and animal burrowing that have disturbed the site over thousands of years. This has been compounded by poor quality records that often emanated from the early excavations and the unavailability of accurate dates that can be scientifically verified.

Nevertheless, new techniques are now in use that were not available to previous researchers. These include digital imaging, 3D mapping and carbon dating that should provide much more information than has been discovered so far. The story of Stonehenge, therefore, continues.

Whether all the mysteries surrounding Stonehenge will ever be resolved is open to question since they go too far back with too little clear evidence available. Perhaps, however, it's as well that some questions remain unanswered, since being able to explain everything would rob the monument of its aura of mystery and its power to fascinate.

Museum Collections and Records

Excavations undertaken so far have already uncovered a huge number of items at Stonehenge and the surrounding site. Most of these items are stored or displayed at the Salisbury Museum or the Wiltshire Museum in Devizes. These museums hold nearly all the key collections from the Twentieth Century excavations, although some of the later ones are still undergoing post-excavation analysis.

Both museums are designated by the Museums, Libraries and Archives Council as being pre-eminent collections of national and international importance. As well as the collections, they have extensive archives, records and a library of antiquarian papers and records setting out the background and detailed history of Stonehenge.

Some items, including John Aubrey's and William Stukeley's papers and manuscripts, are available in the Bodleian Library in Oxford or in Cambridge's Corpus Christi College.

A number of items from the Salisbury Museum and the Wiltshire Museum are on loan to the Stonehenge visitor centre and are displayed there. The visitor centre also has a changing programme of exhibitions and events to illustrate the history and features of Stonehenge. These include the latest audio-visual techniques, interactive maps, reconstructions and demonstrations of ancient skills in an effort to make Stonehenge seem relevant and alive even today.

Stonehenge's Place Within the Landscape

At the time of Stonehenge's construction, the site was surrounded by open chalk grassland that was used by the local people to graze their animals. There were some trees in the area although most of the landscape was reasonably open.

Stonehenge today stands within a rich archaeological background that is largely attributed to early Neolithic, late Neolithic and early Bronze Age developments. The local area contains several prehistoric monuments and over 350 burial mounds, providing important information about the way people lived, how society was organised and the ceremonial and funerary processions at the time.

Other Developments That Are Near Stonehenge

In addition to Stonehenge itself, the local area also has the Stonehenge Cursus, Durrington Walls, Woodhenge, Avebury and Silbury Hill plus numerous other smaller developments. The UNESCO World Heritage Site extends to a large part of this landscape, including many of the sites in addition to Stonehenge itself. They indicate that the whole area was important even before Stonehenge was built and that the construction of so many monuments in the same area suggested a period of intense religious and political rivalry.

The Stonehenge Cursus, sometimes known as the Greater Cursus is an enormous ditch and bank earthworks structure that runs for 1.9 miles (3 kilometres) with the width varying from 330 to 490 feet (100-150 metres). It was constructed between 3630 and 3375 B, making it much older than the main Stonehenge monument.

The Cursus is believed to have been a ceremonial site, being aligned to the sunrise of the spring and autumn equinoxes. Two pits near the east and west ends are also aligned to the midsummer sunrise and sunset, while barrows have been formed within the Cursus.

Wooden Counterpart

Two miles to the north east of Stonehenge is the monument's wooden counterpart — Woodhenge. This was probably built around 2300 BC and was in use until about 1800 BC. The site was originally thought to have been a large burial mound surrounded by a bank and ditch that measured 360 feet (110 metres) in diameter with one entrance to the north east. However, these features have been almost entirely destroyed by ploughing.

Aerial photographs identified dark spots in a wheat field and these were subsequently found to be empty sockets that had held large upright timbers. These post holes were arranged in six concentric oval rings that are marked today by concrete posts. The outermost ring measures 141 by 131 feet (43 by 40 metres) and the longer axis for each ring points towards the winter and summer solstice.

The purpose of Woodhenge is unknown, although it is thought it had a ceremonial use and the banks and ditches were for defence. Some of the timbers may have supported a large roofed building with a courtyard at its centre.

At the centre of the site, the remains of a three-year old child were found. The skull had been split open with an axe, leading researchers to believe the child had been sacrificed.

It is thought that a structure similar to Woodhenge may have been at Stonehenge before it was replaced by the great stone circle and trilithons. Similar structures have been found at Durrington Walls, which is only 230 feet (70 metres) away. These wooden structures may have marked a stage on the path to the more permanent versions found at Stonehenge or may have distinguished the purpose of the different sites — wood indicating life and stone representing the transition to death.

This theory is supported by the finding of bones of pigs at Woodhenge but none at Stonehenge. The presence of these items may indicate the former was a site where feasting took place whereas Stonehenge was not a place for living people.

Durrington Walls

Durrington Walls was originally developed as a large timber circle, measuring 500 metres in diameter, and had a henge added in the late Neolithic or early Bronze Age period. It is thought to have been a complementary monument to Stonehenge and is considered the largest ancient monument of its type in Britain.

The henge is the world's largest and was built around 2500 BC in a single construction phase. The ditch measured over ten metres wide and five metres deep, the material dug from it being used to create a three metre high external bank.

The timber circle was aligned with sunrise at the midwinter solstice and so had the opposite alignment to Stonehenge. However, it is thought that construction of the circle was never completed and the timber posts were removed for use elsewhere.

Evidence of Neolithic houses has been found at Durrington Walls and it is thought that a settlement of up to 1,000 houses accommodating around 4,000 people may have been built there. This may for a time have been the largest village in northern Europe and is thought to have housed the workforce that built Stonehenge.

Avebury Henge and Silbury Hill

Around the same time as Durrington Walls was being developed, the nearby Avebury henge was being constructed over a period of several hundred years. It consisted of a large henge that enclosed a total area of 28.5 metres and had within it a big outer stone circle and two smaller stone circles in the centre of the monument.

The outer circle is the largest megalithic stone circle in the world and originally had about one hundred stones. However, some of these were destroyed by local people in the late Medieval and early Modern periods for religious and practical reasons — they either believed that they were pagan symbols or they needed the stone as a building material.

Close to Avebury is Silbury Hill, an artificial chalk mound that was constructed in stages between 2400 and 2300 BC. At forty metres high and covering about five acres, it is about the size of one of the smaller Egyptian pyramids at Giza and is the tallest man-made mound in Europe.

Although the reason for its construction is not known, it would have taken great technical and organisational skill and a huge amount of labour to build. The hill contains 324,000 cubic yards (248,000 cubic metres) of material and is estimated to have taken eighteen million man hours to complete — the equivalent of 500 hundred men working for fifteen years.

Other Developments at A Time of Transition

Other monuments in the area include Robin Hood's Ball, a large religious and ceremonial causewayed enclosure, and Larkhill, another causewayed enclosure that is now covered by modern, military buildings. These causewayed enclosures were so called due to their ditches being crossed by causeways.

Larkhill was built around 1,150 years before the stones were erected at Stonehenge and comprised two concentric circles of ditches that were constructed in segments and extended to 950 metres in length. Skull fragments found in the ditches indicate the site was used as a mortuary while the remains of smashed bowls and cattle bones suggest that feasting took place there. Its discovery in 2016 implies that there are other prehistoric monuments in the area that are still to be found.

Many of these developments occurred at a time of immense religious transition and resulted in great changes to many of the sites. This coincided with the start of what prehistorians refer to as the 'Beaker Culture' when new people, cultures and traditions arrived in Britain.

The Influence of the Beaker People

The Beaker culture, more formally known as the Bell Beaker culture, was so-called because of the shape of the pottery that was often found in their round barrow graves. The Beaker people are believed to have originated in the copper-using area around the Tagus estuary in Portugal about 2800-2700 BC.

The Beakers spread throughout Europe, often along trade routes to distribute goods such as axes. Wherever they settled, they operated as farmers, archers and metal smiths, working in copper and gold before moving to bronze at the start of the Bronze Age period. They generally exerted some influence where they lived, not only in goods and trade but also in terms of religion, culture and ideology.

When they arrived in Britain, they were the first metal smiths, made their own pottery and woven garments, and introduced alcoholic drinks. More relevant to Stonehenge, they were the first to cremate their dead and conduct individual burials in the barrows that were so prevalent in the Stonehenge landscape. Each barrow grave was filled with burial goods, such as daggers, jewellery and pottery, to accompany the dead to the afterlife.

Evidence of these burial practices has been found extensively at Stonehenge and the surrounding area. The stone circles erected during the late Neolithic and early Bronze Age period are also attributed to the Beaker people and this is perhaps their biggest legacy for Britain.

The Beaker culture was also part of the changeover from the late Neolithic to the early Bronze Age period. At the same time, Stonehenge was being transformed to incorporate the massive sarsen stones with lintels that we see today.

The Amesbury Archer — The King of Stonehenge?

One particularly interesting find, in the spring of 2002 while preparing land for the construction of a school, was the discovery of the grave of a man who was to become widely known as the 'Amesbury Archer'. The grave contained not only the remains of the man but also golden artefacts and other items that made it the richest Bronze Age burial site yet found up to that time.

The grave is about two miles south east of Stonehenge and not far from Durrington Walls. Analysis of the remains suggests the man originated from central Europe while some pottery and jewellery found on the burial site appear to be of European origin.

The items found there include a wrist guard that indicated the archer's high status, a copper knife, Beaker pots, arrow heads and gold jewellery. The quality and quantity of the items in the grave, amounting to almost one hundred pieces, are far greater than those found at comparable sites and indicate the man must have possessed great wealth and power.

Radiocarbon dating of the remains indicates that the man lived between 2400 and 2200 BC, around the time the huge stone circles and the avenue to the River Avon were being built. This, combined with the Archer's origins and obvious wealth, have led to some naming him the 'King of Stonehenge', believing he was part of a ruling elite. There is, however, no real evidence to support this belief.

Military Connections

The modern buildings that were starting to encroach on the site in the 1920s have long been removed. As recently as one hundred years ago, however, a First World War airfield was built in the area between the current visitor centre and the ancient stones.

Pilots were trained there before being transferred to the Western Front. Consequently, fighter planes flew constantly around the monument and there were incidences of crashes near the site.

The Salisbury Plain area has long had links with the military, with records showing Royal Engineers reconnaissance balloons taking part in exercises there from the 1880s and the War Office acquiring areas of land around the monument. Thankfully, all signs of the airfield have long since been removed and Stonehenge has been left in relative peace.

Stonehenge Folklore

Given Stonehenge's long history and the general air of mystery that surrounds the monument, it is hardly surprising that a number of myths are associated with it.

One of the tales stems from a belief that Stonehenge was built as a memorial to slain nobles. This was put forward by Geoffrey of Monmouth in the Twelfth Century, in his book History of the Kings of Britain, and gives a more unlikely explanation of the way Stonehenge was built.

He believed Stonehenge's stones were healing rocks that had been brought to Ireland from Africa by giants. Stonehenge was chosen in the Fifth Century as the site for a memorial to 3,000 nobles killed by the

Saxons in battle. King Aurelius Ambrosius sent Merlin, his brother and King Arthur's father Uther Pendragon and 15,000 knights to Ireland to retrieve the stones.

Merlin's Magic Moves the Stones

They killed 7,000 Irish in the attempt but could not move the stones. Merlin, however, succeeded by magical means and transported the stones on ships to England where they were erected at Stonehenge. King Aurelius Ambrosius and others were buried there. If this tale were true, it would have Stonehenge being built some 2,000 years after the generally accepted date.

An alternative legend relates the treacherous killing of 420 Brythonic warriors by invaders led by King Hengist. Full of remorse for the deed, Hengist erected Stonehenge as a monument.

The Legend of the Heel Stone

A related folk tale concerns the Heel Stone, also previously known as the 'Friar's Heel' or the 'Sun Stone' — the latter probably a reference to the fact that sunrise at the summer solstice is over the stone when viewed from the stone circle. The tale tells how the Devil bought the stones from a woman in Ireland and brought them to Salisbury Plain.

The stones were supposedly obtained by trickery, the Devil promising to pay the woman as much gold as she could count in the time it took him to move them. In fact, since he moved them instantly to England by magical powers, the woman had no time to count any gold and the Devil got the stones for nothing.

Although one stone fell in the River Avon, the rest arrived safely and the Devil proclaimed that no-one would ever discover their source or, depending on the version of this tale, would be unable to count the number of stones. Hearing a friar cast doubt on this, the Devil threw a stone that hit the friar on a heel and then stuck in the ground, where it remains today.

This tale has been attributed to Geoffrey of Monmouth although his account of the building of Stonehenge bears little resemblance. Though the story is, of course, pure fiction, the Heel Stone does bear what many people see as the imprint of a foot.

Giants and Aliens

One theory about Stonehenge is that it was built by giants, the Nephilin, who were almost completely wiped out by the flood associated with Noah and his ark. They used their great height and strength to transport and erect the stones. This does, to some degree, fit in with the Merlin theory because there is a picture from the Fourteenth Century that shows a giant helping Merlin to build Stonehenge.

There is, however, no physical evidence to support this and it can be dismissed as just another myth. Also easily dismissed is a story that the stones at Stonehenge are actually composed of giants who were turned to stone while dancing round in a circle.

One of the most bizarre explanations of how Stonehenge was built is that God-like aliens provided the necessary knowledge to mankind. This know-how was apparently also used to build many other huge ancient structures, including the Moai heads on Easter Island and the pyramids in Egypt.

Whilst all of these tales are barely credible as being real, they do often reflect the beliefs prevalent at the time and may have at least some small basis of truth behind them. None of them, however, can detract from the mystery that continues to surround Stonehenge.

Stonehenge Today

Stonehenge is now a major tourist attraction that has visitors from all around the world. It is a World Heritage Site, is owned by the Crown and managed by English Heritage, with the surrounding land being owned by the National Trust, and has been a legally protected Scheduled Ancient Monument since 1882. It seems, therefore, that its future is safe although that does not mean it is free from argument and controversy — far from it.

Access to the stones has been restricted since 1977, with visitors only allowed within them at the summer and winter solstices or through special bookings. Traffic is also kept away, so tourists make the 1.5 mile (2.1

kilometres) journey from the visitor centre either on foot or by shuttle bus. This is combined with a timed ticketing system that in theory prevents too many visitors being on site at any one time and should ensure a more enjoyable experience.

The shuttle buses replaced a previous fleet of road trains — carriages pulled by Land Rovers. These were taken out of service because of difficulties turning at the monument and the visitor centre, allegedly due to the carriage doors being on the wrong side to allow easy alignment with the platforms.

The New Visitor Centre and The Dangers of Over-Commercialisation

The visitor centre itself is relatively new, being opened in 2013 at a cost of £27 million. It replaced previous facilities that were less than adequate, comprising an unwelcoming building, portable toilets and a grim tunnel under the road to get to the site. The new centre is a state-of-the-art building that includes the usual ticket area, café and obligatory gift shop plus exhibitions and displays that aim to educate and familiarise visitors with Stonehenge's background and history.

Since Stonehenge attracted over 1.3 million visitors in 2016, a 1.1% increase on the previous year, the whole approach can be viewed as a great success. Nevertheless, it has its share of critics, many of whom focus on the over-commercialisation of the site.

If that is true, it is perhaps typified by the replica Neolithic houses that have been constructed behind the visitor centre. These are intended to illustrate how people lived 4,500 years ago and were supposedly built using authentic materials and techniques. There are also demonstrations of ancient domestic skills, such as grinding grain and making ropes — but the whole thing is step too far for some people who prefer a more authentic experience.

The Problem of the Roads

One of the big problems associated with
Stonehenge has long been the proximity of
two increasingly busy roads — the A344
between Andover and Warminster to the
north and the A303 Basingstoke to Honiton
road to the south. The roads were part of the
problem mentioned in a National
Geographic Condition Survey published in
2006, which rated the monument 75th among
94 leading World Heritage Sites and said it
was 'in moderate trouble'.

Both roads run close to the stones and, since
Stonehenge became a World Heritage Site,
there have been plans to upgrade the A303
and to close the A344 so that the view from
the stones is improved. Re-routing of the
roads is expensive and so many schemes

have been suggested and cancelled over the years. However, approval of the new visitor centre, granted by the government in 2009, was coupled with the closure of the A344.

Planning permission for the centre was granted by Wiltshire Council the following year and the centre was subsequently built with the help of a £10 million Heritage Lottery Fund grant. Shortly before the new visitor centre opened, the A344 was closed on 23rd June 2013 and work started to remove it and re-grass the area.

The latest plan to alleviate traffic problems is now focused on the A303. This is the main trunk road from London to the West Country and runs within 165 metres of the monument. It is single carriageway at this point, creating a bottleneck with inherent pollution and noise, that restricts access on foot to the surrounding landscape.

The Controversy of the Proposed Tunnel

On 12th June 2017, Transport Secretary Chris Grayling announced plans to convert the A303 to dual carriageway and, at an estimated cost of £1.4 billion, to take the road through a tunnel under the site. The 1.7-mile-long tunnel is part of an overall road improvement plan that aims to create a more effective link between the A303, M3 and M5 as well as improving traffic flow and benefiting the local economy, at a total cost of £2 billion.

The tunnel is an old idea, first suggested in 1989, but the latest version has been hailed by Historic England as an investment in the country's heritage. The UNESCO World Heritage organisation has approved the plan in principle and the move is supported by English Heritage and the National Trust, who both believe it will improve the understanding and enjoyment of the monument. Nevertheless, there are plenty of critics of the proposed development.

There are fears that, given that the new road will be wider and will have slip roads, the actual road surface within the site will actually be greater. An alternative suggestion is to make the existing A303 a one-way road westbound and build an eastbound route some distance from Stonehenge. This will be much less expensive and will reduce by half the volume of traffic but seems unlikely to get the go-ahead.

Historians and archaeologists believe the tunnel could cause damage to the monument and the overall landscape while others think it is a mistake to try and reverse history. They argue that the A303 is now part of the Stonehenge environment and its existence should not be ignored by grassing over the existing road and hiding the new one. That would be trying to turn the clock back to times gone by and attempting to create a landscape that is thought to be 'authentic' for the site, which is an impossible dream.

There is even an opinion that tunnelling the road will unfairly hide the stones from the travelling public and the only way they will get to see them is by paying an entrance fee to the site. It seems obvious that whatever is done will not please everyone and that may simply be a continuation of Stonehenge's mysterious and sometimes controversial past.

Made in the USA
San Bernardino, CA
30 December 2019